Design: Jill Coote

Recipes: D.M. Arnot, Ann Hohren, Rosie Brook,

Joan Davies, Chris Hardisty, Freda Hooter,

Pam Knutson, Vivien Margison, Alison Ray

Recipe Photography: Peter Barry

Recipe Styling: Bridgeen Deery and Helen Burdett

Jacket and Illustration Artwork: Jane Winton,

courtesy of Bernard Thornton Artists, London

Compiled and introduced by Laura Potts

Edited by Josephine Bacon

Published by
CHARTWELL BOOKS, INC.
A Division of **BOOK SALES, INC.**
110 Enterprise Avenue
Secaucus, New Jersey 07094

CLB 3351

© 1993 CLB Publishing,

Godalming, Surrey, England

Printed and bound in Singapore

All rights reserved

ISBN 1-55521-977-2

THE LITTLE BOOK ·OF·

Vegetarian

RECIPES

An appealing collection of tasty and nutritionally well-balanced vegetarian recipes.

CHARTWELL
BOOKS, INC.

Introduction

If you were to ask a cross-section of the population what they envisaged when they thought of vegetarian food, a large proportion would still describe it as bland and unimaginative, consisting of unappealing dishes made with lentils, and little else. Sadly this inaccurate image is one that has dogged vegetarian cuisine for many years, and appears hard to shake off. In truth, vegetarian cooking is neither bland nor unimaginative. At its very best, it is a subtle, tasty and innovative combination of textures and flavors. It employs ingredients that are often neglected in conventional cooking, such as beans, pulses, grains, and nuts, and uses to full effect a wide range of fresh vegetables.

Vegetarianism has grown in popularity over the past few years, and the reasons for this are varied. For many, the decision to have a meat-free diet is based on the belief that it is morally wrong to kill animals for food, while others choose to give it up as a protest against modern factory farming methods. A significant number, however, choose to adopt a vegetarian diet because they believe that it is better for their health. Today's diet, which is high in animal proteins, reflects the affluence of our society. Whereas our forefathers ate meat infrequently and in relatively small amounts, supplementing it with alternative forms of protein, like beans and pulses, we eat meat on a far more regular basis, and in larger quantities. It is thought that the increase in consumption of cholesterol-rich animal proteins may play a part in the increased prevalence of coronary-related diseases. This has led many people to cut down on their consumption of animal products, particularly red meat, which are known to be high in cholesterol.

Whatever your diet, it is vital to ensure that your body gets all the essential proteins and minerals that it needs. Animal products, such as meat, fish, eggs, and dairy foods, conveniently provide all the amino acids – the building blocks from which proteins are formed – needed by the body. Vegetable proteins, while rich in amino acids, do not contain all of them. Different groups of vegetable proteins, such as grains, nuts, and legumes (beans), contain different amino acids, so complementing each other. By combining different types of vegetable and dairy products, it is possible to maintain the correct balance. A dish like Macaroni Cheese is a good example of how a non-meat dish can be put together to ensure the correct balance of protein.

You don't have to be a firmly committed vegetarian to enjoy vegetarian cookery, and these recipes are designed for the enjoyment of vegetarian and non-vegetarian alike. Using a wide variety of ingredients to create tasty, yet nutritionally well-balanced meals, they show just how versatile vegetarian cooking can be.

Wild Rice Soup

SERVES 4

A meal in itself when served with wholewheat bread and a green salad.

Preparation: 15 mins
Cooking: 30 mins plus 40 mins for the wild rice

¼ cup wild rice
2 cups water
2 onions, chopped
1 tbsp unsalted butter
2 sticks celery, chopped
½ tsp dried thyme
½ tsp dried sage
3¾ cups water or vegetable broth
2 tsps vegetable extract or Maggi seasoning
1 tbsp soy sauce
6 small potatoes, peeled and roughly chopped
1 carrot, finely diced
Milk or single cream

---

1. Add the wild rice to the water, bring to the boil, reduce the heat, and simmer 40-50

Step 2 Sauté the onions in the butter until transparent.

Step 8 Add the milk or cream to thin the soup to the desired consistency.

minutes until the wild rice has puffed and most of the liquid has been absorbed.

2. Sauté the onions in the butter until transparent.

3. Add the celery, thyme, and sage and cook 5-10 minutes.

4. Add the water, vegetable extract, soy sauce, and potatoes.

5. Simmer 20 minutes or until the potatoes are cooked.

6. Blend the mixture in a liquidizer until smooth.

7. Return to the pan, add the carrot and wild rice.

8. Add the milk or cream to thin the soup to the desired consistency.

9. Reheat gently and serve.

Fennel and Walnut Soup

SERVES 4

A delicious soup perfect for special occasions.

PREPARATION: 15 mins
COOKING: 1 hr 10 mins

1 bulb fennel, chopped
1 head celery, chopped
1 large onion, chopped
1 tbsp olive or sunflower oil
3 tbsps walnuts, crushed
5 cups vegetable broth
3 tbsps Pernod
⅔ cup single cream
Salt and pepper
Parsley to garnish

Step 3
Liquidize the simmered ingredients together and return to the pan.

Slice the fennel bulb in half and then roughly chop.

1. Sauté the fennel, celery, and onion in the oil over a low heat 10 to 15 minutes.

2. Add the crushed walnuts and the broth and simmer 30 minutes.

3. Liquidize the simmered ingredients together and return to the pan.

4. Add the Pernod, single cream, and salt and pepper.

5. Reheat gently making sure that it does not boil. Serve garnished with parsley.

Cream of Carrot Soup

SERVES 4

A classic soup which is suitable for any occasion.

PREPARATION: 10 mins
COOKING: 35 mins

---

1 large onion, chopped
2 cloves garlic, crushed
1 tbsp olive oil
1 pound carrots, chopped
1 tsp mixed herbs
3¾ cups vegetable broth
⅔ cup sour cream
Salt and pepper

Step 2 Add the carrots, mixed herbs and broth.

Step 3 Bring to the boil and simmer about 30 minutes until the carrots are soft.

1. Sauté the chopped onion and garlic in the oil until transparent.

2. Add the carrots, mixed herbs, and broth.

3. Bring to the boil and simmer about 30 minutes until the carrots are soft.

4. Cool a little and then liquidize until smooth.

5. Add the sour cream, season to taste, and mix thoroughly.

6. Heat through gently, making sure the soup does not boil, and serve.

Watercress and Mushroom Pâté

SERVES 4
A delightful pâté served with thinly-sliced brown bread.

PREPARATION: 10 mins
COOKING: 5 mins

2 tbsps butter
1 medium onion, finely chopped
½ cup dark, flat mushrooms, finely chopped
1 bunch watercress, finely chopped
½ cup small curd cottage cheese
Few drops soy sauce
Scant ½ tsp caraway seeds
Black pepper

1. Melt the butter over a low heat and cook the onion until soft but not colored.

Step 3 Add the chopped watercress and stir about 30 seconds until it becomes limp.

Step 7 Pour into individual ramekin dishes or one large serving dish and chill for 2 hours.

2. Raise the heat, add the mushrooms and cook quickly 2 minutes.

3. Add the chopped watercress and stir about 30 seconds until it becomes limp.

4. Place the contents of the pan in a blender together with the cottage cheese and soy sauce.

5. Blend until smooth, stirring the mixture if necessary.

6. Stir in the caraway seeds and pepper to taste.

7. Pour into individual ramekin dishes or one large serving dish and chill for at least 2 hours until firm.

Red Lentil Soufflé

SERVES 4

Serve this tasty soufflé with watercress or salad

PREPARATION: 15 mins
COOKING: 40 mins

½ cup red lentils
1 bayleaf
1¼ cups water
2 tbsps margarine or butter
6 tbsps heavy cream
2 large egg yolks
3 large egg whites
2 tbsps grated yellow cheese (optional)
Salt and pepper
Pinch of paprika

---

1. Pick over the lentils and remove any stones. Rinse well.

2. Place the lentils, bayleaf, and water in a pan and bring to the boil.

Step 1 Pick over the lentils and remove any stones.

Step 6 Beat the egg whites until very stiff and fold into the mixture.

3. Simmer 20 minutes or until the lentils are soft.

4. Remove the bayleaf and purée the lentils until they are very smooth.

5. Beat in the margarine, cream, and egg yolks.

6. Beat the egg whites until very stiff and fold into the mixture.

7. Season and fold in the grated cheese.

8. Pour into a well-greased soufflé dish and sprinkle with a little paprika.

9. Bake in a preheated 375°F oven for approximately 20 minutes or until the soufflé is well risen, firm, and brown.

10. Serve immediately.

Mushrooms and Tofu in Garlic Butter

SERVES 4

A quick and delicious starter.

PREPARATION: 10 mins
COOKING: 12 mins

---

2 cups button mushrooms
1 inch root ginger
1 cup smoked tofu
½ cup butter
2 small cloves garlic, crushed
2 tbsps chopped parsley

---

1. Wipe the mushrooms with a damp cloth.

2. Peel and grate the root ginger.

3. Cut the smoked tofu into ½-inch squares.

Step 7 Add the smoked tofu and heat through.

Step 2 Peel and grate the root ginger.

4. Melt the butter in a skillet.

5. Add the crushed garlic and ginger and fry gently two minutes.

6. Add the mushrooms and cook gently 4-5 minutes until the mushrooms are softened.

7. Finally, add the smoked tofu and heat through.

8. Divide between 4 pre-heated bowls, sprinkle with chopped parsley and serve at once with French bread or crusty wholewheat rolls.

Cauliflower and Broccoli Souflettes

SERVES 6

Serve as a wintertime starter or as a main meal with rice salad and ratatouille.

PREPARATION: 15 mins
COOKING: 50 mins

2 cups cauliflower
2 cups broccoli
4 tbsps margarine
½ cup brown rice flour
2 cups milk
¼ cup grated yellow cheese
1 large egg, separated
Good pinch of nutmeg

1. Break the cauliflower and broccoli into small flowerets and steam until just tender - about 7-10 minutes.

2. Melt the margarine, remove from the heat, and gradually add the flour. Stir to make a roux

Step 1 Break the cauliflower and broccoli into small flowerets and steam until just tender.

Step 7 Divide the sauce evenly between the ramekin dishes.

and add the milk gradually, blending well to ensure a smooth consistency.

3. Return the pan to the heat and stir until the sauce thickens and comes to the boil.

4. Cool a little and add the egg yolk and cheese, stir well, and add nutmeg to taste.

5. Whip the egg white until stiff and fold carefully into the sauce.

6. Place the vegetables into 6 small greased ramekin dishes and season.

7. Divide the sauce evenly between the dishes and bake immediately in a preheated 375°F oven about 35 minutes until puffed and golden.

8. Serve at once.

Wheatberry Salad

SERVES 4

This makes a substantial salad dish which provides an almost perfect protein balance.

PREPARATION: 20 mins

1 cup wheatberries, cooked
½ cup red beans, cooked
3 medium tomatoes, sliced
4 green onions (scallions), chopped
2 sticks celery, chopped
1 tbsp pumpkin seeds

Dressing
4 tbsps olive or sunflower oil
2 tbsps red wine vinegar
1 clove garlic, crushed
1 tsp grated fresh ginger root
1 tsp paprika
1 tbsp soy sauce
Fresh or dried oregano, to taste
Ground black pepper

Step 1 Mix the salad ingredients together in a large bowl.

2. Shake the dressing ingredients together in a screw-topped jar or combine in a blender.

3. Pour over the salad and toss gently.

Step 3 Pour the prepared dressing over the salad.

1. Mix the salad ingredients together, reserving a few pumpkin seeds and green onions for garnish.

Sunset Salad

SERVES 4-6

Serve this colorful salad with cold nut roasts, pies, or quiche.

3 dessert apples
1 head celery, trimmed
4 medium mushrooms
⅓ cup walnuts
Lettuce leaves
⅓ cup alfalfa sprouts
⅓ cup black grapes

Dressing
½ cup mayonnaise
¼ cup plain yogurt
Seasoning

Step 6 Line the serving dish with well-washed lettuce and spread the sprouts around the outer edge.

Step 1 Cut the unpeeled apples into quarters and remove the cores.

1. Cut the unpeeled apples into quarters and remove the core. Dice roughly.

2. Dice the celery and slice the mushrooms.

3. Chop the walnuts into quarters.

4. Mix the mayonnaise and yogurt together and season.

5. Put the apples, celery, mushrooms, and walnuts into a bowl and fold in the dressing.

6. Line a serving dish with well-washed lettuce and spread the sprouts around the outer edge.

7. Pile the salad in the center and garnish with grapes.

Carrot and Cashew Nut Roast

SERVES 6

A delicious roast to serve hot, but the full flavor is more prominent when the roast is served cold.

PREPARATION: 20 mins
COOKING: 1 hr 10 mins

---

1 medium onion, chopped
1-2 cloves garlic, crushed
1 tbsp olive or sunflower oil
1 pound carrots, cooked and mashed
½ cup cashew nuts, ground
½ cup wholewheat breadcrumbs
1 tbsp light tahini
1½ tsps caraway seeds
1 tsp yeast extract*
Juice of ½ a lemon
6 tbsps broth from the carrots or water
Salt and pepper

---

1. Sauté the onion and garlic in the oil until soft.

2. Mix together with all the other ingredients and season to taste.

3. Place the mixture in a greased 2-pound loaf pan.

4. Cover with foil and bake at 350°F 1 hour.

*Yeast extract is available from the gourmet section of the supermarket.

Step 2 Mix the cooked onion and garlic with all the other ingredients.

5. Remove the foil and bake a further 10 minutes.

6. Leave to stand in the baking pan at least 10 minutes before unmolding.

Step 3 Place the mixture in a greased 2-pound loaf pan.

Winter Crumble

SERVES 4-6

*A variety of hearty vegetables topped with oats and cheese
makes the perfect winter meal.*

PREPARATION: 20 mins
COOKING: 1 hr 5 mins

Topping
6 tbsps butter or margarine
1 cup wholewheat flour
½ cup fine oatmeal
½ cup grated yellow cheese
¼ tsp salt

Filling
¾ cup broth or water
1¼ cups sweet cider or apple juice
1 tsp brown sugar
2 carrots, chopped
2 large parsnips, cut into rings
2 sticks celery, chopped
2 heads broccoli, cut into flowerets
¼ cauliflower, cut into flowerets
1 tbsp wholewheat flour
2 tbsps chopped parsley
1 medium onion, chopped and fried
4 large tomatoes, skinned and chopped
1 cup cooked black-eyed peas

1. Make the topping by rubbing the butter into
the flour and oatmeal until the mixture
resembles fine breadcrumbs. Stir in the cheese
and salt.

Step 1 Rub the
butter into the
flour and
oatmeal until
the mixture
resembles fine
breadcrumbs.

2. Mix the stock with the cider and sugar and
put into a large pan with the carrots and
parsnips.

3. Cook until just tender, remove the
vegetables and put aside.

4. Add the celery, broccoli, and cauliflower to
the pan, cook until tender, remove and reserve.

5. Mix the flour with a little water, add to the
cider, and cook until thickened, stirring all the
time. Add the parsley.

6. Place the onions, vegetables, tomatoes, and
beans in a greased casserole and season well.
Pour the sauce over the mixture.

7. Sprinkle the topping over the top and press
down a little.

8. Cook in a preheated 400°F oven 30-35
minutes or until the topping is golden-brown.

Ratatouille Pie with Cheese and Peanut Pastry

SERVES 4-6

A colorful dish to make in the fall when eggplant and zucchini are inexpensive and plentiful.

PREPARATION: 30 mins
COOKING: 1 hr

Ratatouille
2 tbsps olive oil
2 onions, minced
4 tomatoes, skinned and chopped
1 eggplant, diced
3 zucchini, finely sliced
2 sticks celery, chopped

White sauce
½ cup all-purpose flour
4 tbsps margarine
2 cups milk

Dough
4 tbsps butter
1 cup self-rising flour
¼ cup finely grated cheese
¼ cup finely chopped salted peanuts
Milk
Beaten egg

1. Put the oil and all the vegetables into a large pan and cook gently for about 20 minutes or until soft.

Step 6 Place the dough on top of the ratatouille mixture and trim the edges.

2. Melt the margarine in a separate pan and stir in the flour. Gradually add the milk and bring to boiling point stirring all the time.

3. Stir the sauce into the vegetable mixture and put into an ovenproof dish.

4. Rub the butter into the flour and add the cheese and peanuts.

5. Add a little milk and roll out the dough.

6. Place on top of the ratatouille mixture, trim, and brush with beaten egg.

7. Bake in a preheated 375°F oven about 30 minutes or until golden-brown.

Quick Vegetable Chili

SERVES 4

Serve this tasty chili with wholemeal baps and salad.

PREPARATION: 15 mins
COOKING: 30 mins

2 large onions, sliced
1 tbsp olive oil
1 clove garlic, crushed
1 tsp chili powder
1 × 14 ounce can tomatoes, chopped
1 × 14 ounce can of red beans
1 small red bell pepper, chopped
1 medium zucchini, sliced
½ small cauliflower
2 carrots, chopped
½ tbsp tomato paste
1 tsp dried, sweet basil
1 tsp oregano
1 cup broth

1. Sauté the onions in the oil until soft.

2. Add the garlic and cook for 1 minute.

3. Add the chili powder and cook a further minute.

Step 3 Add the chili powder and cook for a further minute.

4. Add the rest of the ingredients and simmer 25-30 minutes.

5. Serve on a bed of brown rice.

Step 4 Add the rest of the ingredients and simmer for 25-30 minutes.

Tomato and Pepper Quiche

SERVES 4

Quiche is tastiest served with baked potatoes and a crisp salad.

PREPARATION: 25 mins
COOKING: 55 mins

Pastry case
1 cup wholewheat flour
Pinch of salt
4 tbsps vegetable fat
A little cold water to mix

Filling
2 tbsps butter or margarine
1 onion, minced
½ green bell pepper, finely sliced
½ red bell pepper, finely sliced
2 tomatoes, finely sliced
3 eggs
1¼ cups single cream
Seasoning
2 tbsps Parmesan cheese

1. Mix the flour and salt together.

2. Cut the fat into small pieces and rub into the flour until the mixture resembles fine breadcrumbs.

3. Add the water and mix until a ball of dough is formed.

4. Roll out to line a 8-inch pie pan.

Step 8 Arrange the onion and pepper on the bottom of the pie pan.

5. Prick the bottom lightly with a fork and bake in a preheated 350°F oven 15 minutes.

6. Remove from the oven.

7. Meanwhile, melt the butter or margarine in a skillet and sauté the onion and pepper until just softened.

8. Arrange the onion and pepper on the bottom of the pie pan, followed by the sliced tomatoes.

9. Beat the eggs, and add the cream and seasoning.

10. Pour over the vegetables and sprinkle the cheese on top.

11. Return to the oven for 35-40 minutes until risen and golden-brown on top.

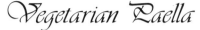

Vegetarian Paella

SERVES 4-6

Perfect served with crusty bread and a green salad.

PREPARATION: 20 mins
COOKING: 45 mins

4 tbsps olive oil
1 large onion, chopped
2 cloves garlic, crushed
½ tsp paprika
1½ cups long-grain brown rice
5 cups broth
¾ cup dry white wine
1 × 14 ounce can tomatoes
1 tbsp tomato paste
½ tsp tarragon
1 tsp basil
1 tsp oregano
1 red bell pepper, roughly chopped
1 green bell pepper, roughly chopped
3 sticks celery, finely chopped
1 cup mushrooms, washed and sliced
¼ cup snow peas, topped and tailed
¼ cup frozen peas
¼ cup cashew nut pieces
Salt and pepper

1. Heat the oil and sauté the onion and garlic until soft.

2. Add the paprika and rice and continue to cook 4-5 minutes until the rice is transparent. Stir occasionally.

Step 2 Add the paprika and rice and continue to cook 4-5 minutes until the rice is transparent.

3. Add the stock, wine, tomatoes, tomato paste, and herbs and simmer 10-15 minutes.

4. Add the pepper, celery, mushrooms, and snow peas and cook another 30 minutes.

5. Add the peas, cashew nuts, and seasoning to taste. Heat through.

6. Garnish with parsley, lemon wedges, and olives.

Step 5 Add the peas, cashew nuts, and seasoning to taste.

Millet Medley

SERVES 4

A tasty and wholesome recipe for the whole family.

PREPARATION: 10 mins
COOKING: 40 mins

---

1 medium onion, chopped
2 tbsps oil
1 cup millet
2½ cups broth or water
Salt and pepper
½ cup cooked peas
½ cup sweetcorn
4 sticks celery, chopped
¼ cup sunflower seeds
2 tbsps soy sauce

---

1. Sauté the onion in the oil 2-3 minutes.

Step 3 Add the broth and seasoning, bring to the boil, and simmer over a low heat 30 minutes.

Step 6 Cook the sunflower seeds and soy sauce over a low heat until the seeds are dry.

2. Add the dry millet and cook a few minutes, stirring all the time.

3. Add the stock and seasoning, bring to the boil, and simmer over a low heat 30 minutes.

4. Allow to cool.

5. Add the peas, sweetcorn, and celery and mix well.

6. Place the sunflower seeds and soy sauce in a skillet and cook over a medium heat, stirring continuously until the seeds are dry. Cool.

7. Just before serving, sprinkle with the toasted sunflower seeds.

Piper's Pie

SERVES 4

This attractive dish makes the perfect family meal.

PREPARATION: 20 mins
COOKING: 50-60 mins

1 pound potatoes, peeled and diced
¾ cup moong beans
8 ounces leeks
1 onion, sliced
½ tsp dill
1 inch fresh ginger root, chopped or finely
   grated
1 tbsp concentrated apple juice
1 tsp miso

1. Boil the potatoes and mash with a little butter and seasoning.

2. In a separate pan, cover the moong beans with water and boil 15-20 minutes until soft.

Step 3 Put the leeks, onions, dill, ginger, and concentrated apple juice in a greased ovenproof dish.

Step 7 Cover the bean mixture with a layer of mashed potato.

3. Meanwhile, generously butter an ovenproof dish and put in the leeks, onion, dill, ginger, and concentrated apple juice. Mix well.

4. Drain the beans, reserving the cooking liquid, and add to the casserole dish.

5. Dissolve the miso in a little of the bean liquid and mix into the casserole, which should be moist but not too wet.

6. Cover and cook in a preheated 400°F oven 30-45 minutes, stirring and adding a little more bean liquid if necessary.

7. Remove from the oven and cover with a layer of mashed potato.

8. Return to the oven to brown or brown under the broiler.

Fifteen-Minute Goulash

SERVES 4

This quick and easy goulash is best served with baked potatoes.

PREPARATION: 10 mins
COOKING: 15 mins

---

1 onion, finely chopped
1 clove garlic, crushed
2 carrots, diced
3 medium zucchini, diced
2 tbsps olive oil
1 tbsp paprika
Pinch of nutmeg
1 heaped tbsp freshly-chopped parsley
1 tbsp tomato paste
14-ounce can tomatoes
1 cup cooked red beans or 1 × 14oz can of
    beans, drained and rinsed
1 cup cooked white navy beans or 1 × 14oz can,
    drained and rinsed
⅔ cup tomato juice or broth
Salt and pepper
Sour cream or yogurt to serve

---

1. Put the onion, garlic, carrots, and zucchini into a pan with the olive oil and sauté 5 minutes until softened.

2. Stir in the paprika, nutmeg, parsley, and tomato paste.

Step 1 Sauté the onion, garlic, carrots, and zucchini for 5 minutes.

3. Add the rest of the ingredients, except cream or yogurt, and cook over a low heat 10 minutes.

4. Turn onto a hot serving platter and top with a little sour cream or yogurt.

Step 4 Top the goulash with a little sour cream or yogurt.

Index

Cauliflower and Broccoli Souflettes, a tasty appetizer.